The Chumash
of California

Jack S. Williams

The Rosen Publishing Group's
PowerKids Press™
New York

For my daughter, Louise

Published in 2002 by The Rosen Publishing Group, Inc.
29 East 21st Street, New York, NY 10010

Photo and Illustration Credits: Cover and pp. 7, 30, 39 courtesy of Mission San Luis Obispo, photos © Cristina Taccone; p. 27 courtesy of Mission San Luis Obispo, reproduction photo © Cristina Taccone; pp. 1, 3, 4 © Erica Clendening; p. 8 courtesy of National Museum of the American Indian, Smithsonian Institution (25/0001), photo by Katherine Fogden; pp. 10, 12, 29 courtesy of the Ventura County Museum of History & Art (background painting on p. 12 courtesy of Kent Christenson), photos © Cristina Taccone; pp. 14, 21, 24, 33, 36, 52, 55 © Corbis; p. 17 courtesy of National Museum of the American Indian, Smithsonian Institution (N08970), photo by J.P. Harrington; p. 19 courtesy of National Museum of the American Indian, Smithsonian Institution (25/4666), photo by David Heald; p. 22 courtesy of the Albinger Archeological Museum, City of Ventura, CA, photo © Cristina Taccone; p. 35 © Tom Simondi; pp. 41, 46 courtesy of Santa Barbara Mission Archive-Library, reproduction photos © Cristina Taccone; p. 42 © Cristina Taccone; p. 49 © Old Military and Civil Records, National Archives and Records Administration; p. 50 courtesy of Smithsonian Institution (49-393).

Book Design: Erica Clendening

Williams, Jack S.
        The Chumash of California / Jack S. Williams.
            p. cm. — (The library of Native Americans)
        Includes bibliographical references and index.
        Summary: This book highlights some of the major events that have taken place since 1542 involving the Chumash people of the Santa Barbara Channel area and also describes the way they lived before the arrival of Europeans.
        ISBN 0-8239-6426-4
        1. Chumash Indians—History—Juvenile literature 2. Chumash Indians—Social life and customs—Juvenile literature. [1. Chumash Indians. 2. Indians of North America—California.] I. Title. II. Series.
        979.4'0049757—dc21

Manufactured in the United States of America

Contents

The Chumash and Their Neighbors

Salinan

Obispeño

Yokuts

Kern River

Kawaiisu

9

Cuyama

Emigdiano

Kitanemuk

Vanyume

11

Ineseño

7

Purisimeño

8

Barbareño

10

Tataviam

Serrano

6

Santa Barbara Channel

5 Ventureño

4

Gabrieliño
(Tongva)

San Miguel Island

Santa Cruz Island

Cruzeñõ

Anacapa Island

2

Santa Rosa Island

Ajachmen

California

Area of Detail

3

2

1

Pacific Ocean

Key to Cities

1 San Diego
2 Los Angeles
3 San Francisco
4 Oxnard
5 Ventura
6 Santa Barbara
7 Lompoc
8 Solvang
9 San Luis Obispo
10 Ojai
11 Santa María

One

Introducing the Chumash People

The sounds of crashing waves have been heard for hundreds of thousands of years along the shoreline of California. Many different Native American peoples have made their homes by the churning green and blue waters of the Pacific Ocean. None of these groups was more famous than the one we call the Chumash. These Native Americans are known throughout the world for their skills as artists, craftspeople, and seafarers. The missions that the Chumash built are considered some of the most beautiful buildings in the American West.

The Native Americans who are now identified as the Chumash lived in and around the Santa Barbara Channel area and spoke languages from the Hokan language family. Their name comes from the term Michumash, which was used for centuries by some Native American people from the California mainland to refer to those who lived on Santa Cruz Island. The name probably meant "A people who make shell bead money." The European explorers and early settlers who followed usually called these people the Canaliños, which means "A people who live by the channel." In 1891, a researcher named John Wesley Powell used the name Chumash in place of the word Canaliño.

This map shows the locations of the Chumash groups who lived in and around the Santa Barbara Channel area and some of the other Native American groups who lived near them.

No one knows when the first Chumash appeared. Experts think that people from Asia came to North America sometime between 13,000 and 40,000 years ago. They probably crossed into the region using a frozen land bridge that stretched from Siberia to Alaska. Over many generations, the immigrants moved south, slowly filling in the land.

Living in one place allowed the people of the Santa Barbara Channel area to develop many elaborate ways of doing things. For example, they learned how to make many specialized tools, such as canoes, fishhooks, and nets, that allowed them to catch fish and travel in the coastal waters.

By about 8,000 years ago, some of these people had settled in the coastal areas of what would later be called California. They used many tools and methods to make a living from the land and the sea. Because food was so abundant there, they settled in the area.

About 1,000 years ago, a group of these people came to share very similar tools, customs, and beliefs. Some anthropologists, scientists who study groups of people, have called the people of this new culture the Canaliños. Most scholars would agree that there were thousands, if not tens of thousands, of Canaliños. These people had many of the same characteristics as the Chumash. Most scholars and Native Americans believe that the Chumash are the descendants of the Canaliños.

When the Spanish reached the Chumash region in 1542, they were amazed by what they saw. Unlike the native people to the south and the north, these Native Americans lived in large, well-organized villages that included immense houses. The Chumash also made exceptionally beautiful stone carvings and baskets. They built plank canoes and

This modern painting depicts a Chumash traveling through the coastal waters in a plank canoe, or *tomol*. *Tomols* ranged from 8 to 30 feet (2–9 m) long and usually were made using driftwood. Planks were glued in place with a melted mix of pine pitch and asphalt.

frequently traveled more than 20 miles (32 km) to nearby islands. The Spanish also quickly learned to fear and respect the Chumash warriors, who were masters of hit-and-run fighting techniques.

The Chumash and the Europeans developed a long and complex relationship. For more than 200 years, between 1542 and 1769, the Native Americans who lived by the Santa Barbara

The Chumash are famous for their beautiful and intricate baskets. This basketry tray includes a Spanish inscription saying that it was made by a woman named Catarina Ortega. It was made during the mission era between 1772 and 1835.

Channel occasionally traded with the crews of passing ships. Then, in 1769, Spain invaded California. Three years later, the first group of European settlers came to live with the Chumash. Between 1773 and 1821, large numbers of natives became allies and partners of the Europeans. However, some of the Chumash resisted the newcomers. Those who befriended the Spanish were eventually betrayed. After 1821, the Native Americans were taken advantage of by settlers. Everything that they had worked to create and maintain—lands, buildings, and the tens of thousands of cattle and horses that they had raised—was stolen. Many of the Chumash were turned into near-slaves.

As more and more newcomers came, the Chumash were pushed aside. In 1846, the United States conquered California. However, for the Chumash, there was no relief. The new government's policies were even more cruel and brutal than those of Spain and Mexico. The Chumash were ruled by politicians who called for the extermination of all California Native Americans. Marshals and sheriffs rounded up native workers and auctioned them off like animals to the highest bidders. With their land filled with enemies and no weapons available to fight back, there was little that the Chumash could do but hide, or pretend that they were not Indians.

The story of the Chumash and the Europeans is one of accomplishment, lost opportunities, and tragedy. In this book you will learn about some parts of the Chumash story, including the major events that have taken place since 1542, and the way the Chumash lived before the arrival of the Europeans.

Two
Chumash Technology

When Spanish explorers encountered the Chumash in 1542, what did they look like? What kinds of houses did they live in? What kinds of things did they make and use? The Chumash had their own way of doing things. They had unique kinds of settlements, where they produced an amazing collection of objects that were both beautiful and useful. Perhaps most amazing of all, nearly everything that the Chumash had came from the natural world that surrounded them.

Living with Nature

Chumash people were deeply connected to the natural world. From the land they harvested dozens of different kinds of wild plants, including cattail pollen, walnuts, Toyon berries, chamomile, Chia sage seeds, Manzanita berries, Miner's lettuce, pine nuts, seaweed, and rose hips. The Chumash men were also expert hunters—they hunted antelopes, bears, birds, deer, mountain lions, and rabbits.

The sea also produced remarkable opportunities for fishing. The people who lived along the shoreline hunted dolphins, otters, seals,

Natural resources such as minerals, stones, and the bones of animals were used by the Chumash to create tools. These projectile points may have been used as knife blades, arrowheads, or spear points.

and sea lions. They also ate shellfish and dozens of different kinds of fish. Occasionally, dead whales washed onto the beaches. The parts of the animals the Chumash did not eat, such as bones, were used to produce hundreds of useful things, such as furniture, beads, and hammers.

The Chumash also used many different kinds of stones and minerals. They collected tar from pools that formed on the mainland or from lumps that floated onto the beaches. Plants and trees were essential sources of other raw materials.

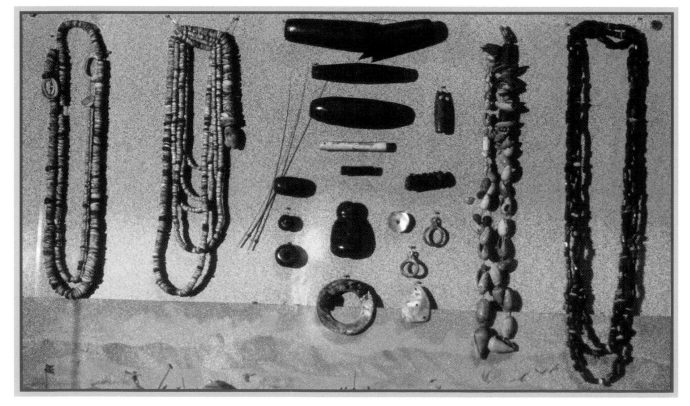

12   Many different kinds of material, such as bone, shell, and stone, were used to make jewelry and other similar items.

Most of the things that the Chumash needed from nature could be found near to their homes. However, they had to trade with other Native American groups for some of their raw materials, such as a red mineral known as hematite and the soft rock known as soapstone.

The attitudes that most Chumash had about using nature were very different from those of Europeans. Many Chumash believed it was essential that the resources be preserved. People who live by hunting and gathering nearly always understand that they must balance their needs with those of other forms of life. The Chumash saw themselves as part of the natural world, rather than as its owner.

Despite their attempts to live in harmony with nature, Native American people still suffered many problems. Disastrous storms, diseases, droughts, and other catastrophes took place. As the population slowly grew, the competition between communities for resources, such as food and water, also increased. Sometimes people were greedy or jealous, or they warred with each other. The ancient Chumash lived in a world of plenty but, like our present-day world, it also was full of conflict.

Clothing and Body Decoration

The climate of the Santa Barbara Channel area is relatively mild. As a result, the Chumash got by with wearing remarkably small amounts of clothing.

The men and young children generally went without clothing. The men wore long hair that was usually tied up in the back, near the tops of their heads. Many men wore a kind of belt, or net bag,

around their waist. When the men went hunting, they sometimes wore whole deerskins as a disguise. Of course, when it was cold, both men and women wrapped themselves in blankets and capes. The Chumash leaders were the only people allowed to wear capes that dropped all the way down to their ankles. Everyone else had to wear shoulder coverings that dropped no lower than their waists.

The women wore more clothing than did the men. Every adult female had a skirt. When they went outside they usually wore a short cape. The women's

Modern ceremonial clothing often reflects many different Native American traditions. This headdress worn by a present-day Chumash is made from seashells, bird down, and feathers.

hairstyles were very different from those of the men. Their long hair was usually allowed to fall over their shoulders. The women wore bangs that were carefully trimmed using pieces of burning tree bark or twigs.

Both men and women occasionally wore sandals made from reeds. Most of the Chumash did not have any kind of protection for their feet. Some people wore hats that were woven like baskets. During celebrations, leaders and dancers sometimes wore elaborate headgear made from bones, seashells, white bird down, and feathers. The people at these events also put on skirts made from milkweed, feathers, and bird down. Other ceremonial dress included feather cloaks and whole animal skins, such as those of bears.

The Chumash used hematite to paint their bodies. Every village had its own set of symbols. By looking at the decorations on someone, a Chumash person could figure out where he or she came from.

Nearly all the Chumash enjoyed wearing jewelry. Items that were popular included hairpins, nose plugs, bead necklaces, pendants, and earrings. Nearly all the adults pierced their ears. Beads were also sewn onto clothing.

Villages and Towns

The lives of the Chumash centered on their villages and towns. There were hundreds of these settlements. Some of the communities consisted of little more than a few houses built around a large, open space. However, many of the larger villages or towns had dozens of houses and many special structures and areas.

Every settlement was built in a place in which there was an adequate supply of flowing water. Most of the communities were created on hillsides or hilltops that overlooked rivers, streams, or springs. Those located on the coast were often built next to sandy beaches. Whenever possible, a village was built near a large, rocky place where acorns and other seeds could be ground.

The average Chumash family lived in a small hut made from poles and bulrushes, or reeds. These houses had circular floor plans and ranged from 10 to 20 feet (3–6 m) in diameter. However, in the larger villages the most important families had immense houses. These structures could be up to 50 feet (15 m) across. Inside, the walls were lined with low, wooden platforms that served as beds. People slept on top of reed mats on the beds. A hole in the center of the roof allowed light to enter the structure and smoke to rise into the sky. When it rained, a piece of animal skin was used to cover the opening. A fire pit, or hearth, was dug in the middle of the room. The flames kept the house warm and provided heat for indoor cooking during bad weather. Most of the time, the people cooked out of doors. In some of the larger homes, mats were used to divide the interior into smaller areas.

In the big towns of the coast, people's homes were organized into neat rows separated by straight paths. The leader's house was surrounded by structures that were used as warehouses. There were also areas where people who made stone tools, jewelry, or canoes would come to work and talk.

Although the Chumash had to work hard, they still had time to do other things. Most settlements had a flat, smooth area that was used for sports. The Chumash loved to play games that were similar to kickball. Low walls made from mats and poles surrounded some sports areas.

This photo shows a larger Chumash home made of poles and bulrushes. Next to it is a frame for another hut.

Each community had a special, sacred area called a *siliyik* that was surrounded by tall walls made from reed mats. Colorful banners fluttered from the flagpoles that surrounded the *siliyik*. The enclosure was usually built in the form of a circle or a semicircle. Inside the *siliyik* the religious leaders of the Chumash held their most sacred ceremonies. On these occasions, most people sat outside the *siliyik*, next to an area used for dancing.

Every village had a sweat lodge. This was a small structure that was partially buried in the ground. Inside a fire produced smoke and heat. To get in and out of the building, people had to use a ladder. Sweat lodges were used for cleaning and healing.

Throughout the settlement, the people set up various kinds of pole and thatch coverings for shade. Reed mats were used to create temporary walls that served as windbreaks.

Almost every village and town had a cemetery. The Chumash buried their dead in graves. They often placed something that had been important to the person on the grave. A painted pole marked every burial place.

The Chumash did not build any kind of walls for their village's defense. When they were at war, the people often took shelter in nearby caves, or on rocky hilltops. If an enemy attacked and burned their village, the Chumash knew that their buildings could be replaced.

Cooking

Food was prepared by Chumash women using a variety of different techniques. Many of the wild plants they ate, such as acorns, had to be ground into powder and soaked in fresh water to remove poisonous substances. Some kinds of shellfish, such as abalone, had to be pounded with stones before they could be cooked. Many items, such as wild cherries, could be eaten fresh, without any preparation.

Most cooking took place over an open flame. Many items were grilled, steamed, or smoked. The Chumash also had stone griddles. Animal fat was used to grease the pan. Some dishes were boiled in stone bowls. The Chumash also knew how to cook food using baskets and hot rocks.

Some foods had to be eaten fresh and were only available during certain seasons. Many provisions were preserved for later use. For example, fish and meat were salted and smoked. Other plant foods were dried in the sun. Because they were able to preserve

The Chumash made knives that helped them to prepare food.

and store so many different kinds of food, it was possible for the Chumash to eat similar meals year-round.

Other Arts and Crafts

The Chumash produced many other kinds of remarkable artwork and crafts. They made hundreds of types of objects of exceptional strength, effectiveness, and beauty.

Stone was one of the Native Americans' most important resources. With chipped stone they produced an amazing variety of objects, including arrowheads, spear points, knives, scrapers, drills, and many other cutting tools. The Chumash also knew how to grind harder stones, such as granite, sandstone, and basalt, into useful things. They created pestles, which were long stone cylinders, to be used with mortars, which were rocks with large, round holes. The men also crafted *manos*, which were small stone tablets, to be used with *metates*, which were slablike pieces of rock. Mortars, pestles, *manos*, and *metates* were used to crack and grind nuts and seeds into flour.

The Chumash did not make pottery. Instead they used a remarkable kind of rock known as soapstone to make smoking pipes, cooking bowls, and griddles. Soapstone was special because, unlike most rocks, it did not crack when it was rapidly heated or cooled. Pieces of soapstone and a similar kind of rock, known as serpentine, were used to make arrow-shaft strengtheners and doughnut-shaped weights for digging sticks.

Many of the things that the Chumash made came from the animals they hunted. Animal skins were used to make clothing and blankets. Bones were turned into gambling sticks, furniture, needles, hairpins, fishhooks, hammers, beads, flutes, panpipes, sweat sticks, whistles, and many other tools. Bird feathers were used to make arrows, capes, banners, dance skirts, and headdresses. Seashells were also important to the Chumash. Abalone shells became bowls, fishhooks, and jewelry.

This elaborate pipe in the shape of a fish was carved out of soapstone and decorated with inlaid shells. Soapstone is a special kind of rock that will not crack when it is quickly heated and cooled.

The Chumash of California

Clamshells were used to make rattles, jewelry, scrapers, and knives. Many other kinds of shells were made into small beads. Sharkskin served as sandpaper. Turtle shells and deer hooves were used to make rattles. Sinew, a kind of muscle, was stripped from the bodies of animals and combined with wood to make bows.

The plant world provided other raw materials. Chumash women are still famous for their baskets. Grass, rushes, and willow shoots were collected and woven into intricate geometric patterns. Sometimes, women would include pictures of animals and people

in their designs. They made many different types of baskets, including trays, bowls, jars, hats, boxes, and seed beaters. Some baskets were waterproofed by coating them with tar. Wood was transformed into canoe paddles, gaming sticks, house beams, hairpins, arrows, bowls, stirring sticks, banner poles, digging sticks, musical instruments, hide scrapers, fence posts, trays, ladles, boxes, harpoons, and many other tools. Wood and basketry were combined to make cradleboards for babies. Pinesap was used as a kind of glue. Giant wild rye and similar large grasses produced stems that became arrows and containers for tobacco. Wild hemp, milkweed, nettles, and yucca plants were turned into strong strings, cords, and ropes, which were used to make nets, bags, belts, and many other woven objects. Walnut shells were combined with tar and beads to make dice.

Plank canoes, or *tomols*, were one of the most remarkable items created by the Chumash men. The boats ranged in size from 12 to 30 feet (3.6–9 m) in length, and held up to twelve adults. Most of the wood for the vessels was collected from the beach. The tree limbs and trunks were split into planks and trimmed using stone tools, sharp shells, and antler hammers. Sharkskin was used to finish the planks before they were glued together with tar. Holes were drilled in the planks using stone tools. The planks were sewn together using heavy milkweed cords. A paint made from pinesap and tar that had been colored red with ochre was used to seal the outside of the canoes. Some boats were also decorated with pieces of abalone shell.

A plank canoe or *tomol* such as this modern reproduction could hold as many as twelve adults.

Three

Other Features of Chumash Life

When Spanish explorers reached the Chumash, the Spanish described people who were different from themselves and other Native Americans in terms of language, social structure, government, trade, and religion.

Language

Scholars classify the language that the Chumash spoke as a part of the Hokan language family. There were at least eight different related language groups, or dialects, spoken by the Chumash. The differences between the dialects spoken at the northern and the southern ends of the Chumash region were as great as the differences between the Spanish and the English languages. A Chumash person could always tell where another Chumash person came from by how he or she spoke.

Social Structure

Every community has some form of social structure. It provides a way of dividing people into groups and assigning them special jobs. Among the Chumash, individuals were assigned to a group based on

The early Chumash created elaborate and beautiful rock art inside caves. Most people believe that this kind of art was related to aspects of Chumash religion.

whether they were men or women, how old they were, how much wealth they had, what they did, and who their parents were.

The smallest social groups were families. The work that was assigned to family members was mostly determined by a person's age and whether he or she was male or female. Chumash families were combined into larger groups called clans. Clan members believed that their founder was an animal, such as a bear, an eagle, or a coyote. Each clan was assigned special jobs. Some of the clans had greater wealth, or were thought to deserve special recognition. The people of the most honored clans selected one of their members to be the village leader, who was called a *wot*. Researchers usually call these people chiefs, or chieftains. Women as well as men served as *wots*. *Wots* enjoyed many special comforts and benefits. Male *wots* were the only Chumash who were allowed to have more than one spouse. Although they collected gifts of all kinds, most of the materials were given back to the other members of the community during religious ceremonies.

The wots were aided by a number of specialists, including religious leaders and doctors. The most important helper was called the *paha*. Some of these men served as message carriers and spies, called *ksen*. One of the most powerful groups in the Chumash community was the *wot's* council of advisers, known as the *antap*. This group usually included the village's doctors, religious singers, dancers, and astrologers.

This 1878 photo shows a male Chumash religious leader. The skirt is made from milk-weed and eagle down. Feathers have been attached to the lower ends of the skirt. The headress is a crown of feathers topped with magpie tails.

27

Government

The basic unit of government of the Chumash was the village or town community. The *wot* and his helpers served as the judges and the police. They organized the religious ceremonies and led the people during times of crisis. Most of the time, the *wots* did not try to tell their followers what to do. Both men and women enjoyed a great deal of freedom.

The different Chumash communities often formed temporary alliances. A few of the chiefs from the larger towns gained control of several villages. These people were called *paqwots*.

Every community was surrounded by territory where its own people had the right to hunt and gather. No one else was allowed to come into these areas without permission.

The Chumash fought two kinds of wars. Men sometimes fought ritual battles. The two sides would meet at a place that was agreed to and exchange insults and arrows. After some of the warriors were killed, one side or the other would usually give in. The Chumash also fought wars by making secret attacks, or ambushes. Occasionally, they would attempt to wipe out an entire village.

Trade

Most of the Chumash villagers depended on trade with their neighbors for some of the things that they needed. Native Americans from the islands were frequently seen on the mainland, exchanging their crafts for goods. The people of the mountains often came to the coast to get seafood, such as dried fish. Native Americans from as far away as the Colorado River came to exchange cotton blankets and pottery for the Chumash's remarkable products. Other items that were brought

Items made by the Chumash, such as these abalone fishhooks, were in demand as items to be traded. The fishhook on the left remains unfinished.

to the region by outsiders included special kinds of stone, animal furs, and hematite. Chumash shell beads and pendants were in great demand. Strings of beads were even used as a kind of money.

Religion

Religion was very important to the Chumash. It helped them to understand their world and figure out what they had to do to have a good life. Most early Chumash looked at the universe very

Chumash elders were responsible for conveying ideas about the creation of the universe to younger generations.

differently from how we do today. The elders taught that the universe has three separate worlds that are stacked like plates, one on top of the other. The uppermost world was filled with powerful gods, such as the Moon and the Sun. The Chumash lived on the middle world, which consisted of land that was surrounded by an ocean. The lower world was filled with dark beings, called *nunashish*, who were dangerous to see.

The Chumash had many other beliefs about the nature of the universe, as well as religious stories about how the world and its creatures came into being and changed over time. Some scholars have called these sacred stories tales and legends. However, to the traditional Chumash, they were, and are, just as real as the stories in other religions' sacred books, such as the Bible and the Koran.

Nearly all the Chumash holidays and rituals were connected to their religion. The Native Americans' lives were filled with ceremonies that marked the journey that people make from birth to death, as well as the changing seasons. One of the most important ideas behind religious worship and holidays was the need to balance all the power that existed in the universe. If the power went out of balance, sickness, death, and destruction would follow.

The Chumash holidays were filled with feasts, dances, trading, rituals, pageantry, sporting events, and gambling. Many Native Americans believed that supernatural forces determined who would win the games. The holidays sometimes went on for five or six days.

One of the most amazing and beautiful Chumash stories involves the creation of humankind. Some elders said that the first Chumash were born from the seeds of plants that were started by the female God Hutash on Santa Cruz Island. When the population grew too large, the noise created bothered Hutash, so she decided to send some of the people to live in the empty mainland, across the Santa Barbara Channel. She made a magic rainbow over which the islanders were supposed to walk. As the people made their way across the sky, some of them fell into the ocean. Hutash felt sorry for these human beings, so she turned them into dolphins to save them from drowning. This is why many Chumash believed that the dolphins were their relatives.

The Chumash often worshiped through songs and dance. Their musical instruments included flutes, rattles, and whistles. Sometimes split pieces of wood called clapper sticks were struck to beat out a rhythm. A piece of wood was tied to the end of a string to make a bullroarer. When it was twirled in the air, the bullroarer sounded sort of like a small helicopter. Many different groups performed special dances. Songs accompanied most of the dances.

To prepare for a ceremony, the Chumash usually decorated their bodies with painted symbols and put on special clothes. Sometimes the dancers wore outfits that made them look like animals. When people danced, they often carried bundles of feathers.

Early Chumash often marked the surfaces of cave walls and rocky outcroppings with symbols. This kind of work is called rock art. Some art was made using paint. These pictures are called pictographs. Other marks were made by pecking away

Chumash pictographs such as these show an amazing set of different symbols.

some of the rocks' surface. This kind of picture is called a petro-glyph. We do not know exactly why the Chumash made rock art. Most people believe that the pictures were created as part of their religion. Some scholars believe that the Chumash used rock art to chart the position of stars and keep track of the passage of time. Other people believe that Chumash rock art was created to give their religious leaders special powers. Because rock art is sacred to many modern Native Americans, it is very important that people show respect when they view it.

We have an incomplete picture of early Chumash religion. There are no books that explain their beliefs. People who were not Chumash recorded many of the descriptions of ceremonies. The traditional people who know the most about this religion have never shared their most important beliefs with outsiders. Even if we knew for certain all the details of the faith of the Chumash, it would not be right to record them here. Many Native American people believe that to do so would be profoundly disrespectful, and that it might even hurt someone. It is extremely important that everyone's religious beliefs and rights be protected.

This replica depicts a typical Chumash home. Most Chumash homes contained a fire pit for warmth or cooking and reed mats that were used as beds.

Four

The Chumash and the Newcomers (1542–1900)

When the Spanish explorer Juan Rodriguez Cabrillo arrived in the Chumash region in 1542, he had orders to discover a route to the Atlantic Ocean and to conquer any wealthy people that he found. His search for a land rich in treasure ended in the Channel Islands. Although some of the Chumash were friendly, others were not. During a skirmish with some warriors at the beach, Cabrillo was badly wounded. He died a short while later. The expedition returned to Mexico with the report that California was a hostile and an unforgiving place.

Other explorers and Spanish merchant ships followed. Apparently the Chumash occasionally saw and even traded with the visitors. We do not have any detailed descriptions about the other things that went on. We do know that throughout most of the Americas, contact with Europeans introduced horrible diseases that may have killed as many as 95 percent of the Native American people. Given the repeated visits of the explorers and the merchants, it is likely that the Chumash suffered many deaths from such illnesses. By the time that Spain invaded California in 1769, the population had probably dropped dramatically, and then increased, as it had throughout much of North America.

Mission Santa Barbara, pictured at left, was the center of a Spanish religious community in California. Spain built missions in the hope of making Native Americans into Spanish citizens and gaining control of California.

The Chumash and the Missions

By the middle of the eighteenth century, Spanish officials had become worried that some other European nation might occupy California. If an enemy had the use of the ports of San Diego and Monterey, they could easily launch invasions of Mexico and Peru, the two territories that were seen as the treasure houses of the Spanish Empire. In 1769, an expedition was sent to take control of the region. Four years later, in 1773, the first outpost of European civilization among the Chumash was established at San Luis Obispo. This settlement was a religious community called a mission.

Spain created this community because King Carlos III wanted to control California. However, he did not have the money, soldiers, or colonists that he needed to conquer and occupy the region. The Spaniards' only hope was to form a bond of friendship with some of the Native Americans. Government officials decided that missions would be built as communities in which Native Americans would gradually become Spanish citizens. This goal required a special sensitivity in working with Native American people. A group of Franciscan priests, headed by Junípero Serra, was placed in charge.

From the Franciscans' point of view, the missions provided an opportunity to share God and to help poor people. The priests were usually patriotic about their role as the king's agents. They also

A statue of Father Junípero Serra stands at Mission San Luis Obispo.

believed that they could take the best of what was found in Europe and combine it with the best of the Native American world. Spanish ideals about government and religion would mesh with the Native American peoples' sense of community and their love of nature. European technology, plants, and animals could make the Native Americans' lives easier. Native American knowledge about California's plants and animals could enrich the lives of the new-comers. The Franciscans' goal was to build a community for God that would improve the futures of both the Spanish and the Chumash.

The Making of the Missions

The mission outpost built at San Luis Obispo was much more than a church with some priests whose job was to tell Native Americans about Christianity. It was an outpost of the Spanish empire that was used as a kind of government agency. The Chumash were intro-duced to many aspects of the European way of life, including a whole range of plants, animals, and tools.

For the mission to exist, some of the Chumash had to be per-suaded to join the new community. Why would a Chumash person want to live in a mission? Being a member of one of the new com-munities offered a number of practical benefits. Spanish newcomers had certain powerful weapons, such as ships, firearms, and leather armor. The Spanish would make good allies in any war. They brought steel knives, axes, dozens of new kinds of food, and animals such as horses, sheep, cattle, mules, and chickens. They also had many things of beauty, including paintings, statues, religious rituals, and powerful music. Many Chumash wanted these things once they saw them.

This photo shows the interior of a room at Mission Santa Barbara in the late nineteenth or early twentieth century, many years after the settlement had been abandoned by the Chumash.

The Chumash of California

Some Chumash may have decided to join the missions because of the Franciscans' preaching. The missionaries were visionaries who offered the Chumash a chance to build a new kind of perfect world, or utopia. Although many Chumash joined for other reasons, some people were probably attracted through religious conversion. However, it is impossible to know how many.

Many Chumash decided to move to the missions, where they were known as neophytes, or new followers. The Chumash *wots* often brought whole villages to the new settlements. Once they had moved, the wots and their relatives continued to serve in important

As some Chumash adopted Christianity, they attended churches such as this one at Mission Santa Barbara.

leadership roles. For many mission Indians, the Franciscans and the Spanish government officials were simply a new kind of *paqwot*. The neophytes often visited their non-Christian relatives and friends. They sometimes persuaded these people, whom the Spanish called gentiles, to come to live with them.

Many of the Chumash rejected the missions. A small number of Christian Native Americans ran away from the mission. Others kept their distance from the newcomers, and preserved whatever they could of their older way of life. Some liked the things that the Europeans brought but did not want to adopt their religion. Many of these people decided to find other ways of dealing with the newcomers. Some came to work for them at the military town that was founded at Santa Barbara in 1782. A few of the Chumash attacked the newcomers and stole from them.

By the end of 1787, it was clear that the Spaniards could not be ignored. New missions had been established at San Buenaventura, Santa Barbara, and La Purísima. The settlements' horses and cattle multiplied. They ate traditional Chumash crops and disrupted many other aspects of the natural environment. Several new sicknesses killed both the neophytes and the gentiles. By 1800, it was becoming harder and harder for the Chumash to live in the Santa Barbara Channel area in a traditional way. Some of the Chumash who had resisted gave up and moved into the missions. Many more traveled eastward into California's Central Valley. A few Chumash managed to live secret lives in the rugged mountains.

Although Spain controlled the coast of the mainland, other nations' sailors freely visited the non-Christian Chumash who lived on the islands of San Miguel, Santa Rosa, Santa Cruz, and Anacapa. Groups of Russians and their allies the Inuits (Native Americans from Alaska) ventured south to hunt sea otters. When they came to the Channel Islands, they attacked the Chumash that lived there. The islanders were gradually killed off or driven to the mainland. Sometimes, the priests from the missions would organize rescue operations to save the remaining islanders.

Working with the Franciscans, the Chumash built magnificent mission buildings at San Luis Obispo, San Buenaventura, Santa Barbara, La Purísima Concepción, and Santa Ynés, which was founded in 1804. They learned European trades, performed Spanish music with their own orchestras, sang religious songs in Spanish, Latin, and Chumash, and became expert farmers and cowboys. The neophytes built homes that were similar to those found at the Spanish settlements.

No Chumash community was more beautiful, or more elaborate, than Santa Barbara Mission. The housing area was twice as big as the largest non-Native American settlement in California. There were many rows of comfortable homes separated by wide streets. A stone and tile aqueduct brought water to the mission. There were warehouses, orchards, hospitals, fountains, dams, mills, and factories that turned out rope, blankets, soap, clothing, furniture, leather, and pottery. The Native Americans wore European-style clothing and had household tools that were identical to the ones found among the Spanish colonists. The mission owned thousands of heads of cattle and grew enough food to support a much larger population. Everyone shared in the products and the harvests. The richness and the beauty of the mission was a direct product of the hard work of the Chumash.

Although people were living comfortably, diseases and other problems were slowly reducing the number of Native Americans who lived in the missions. Conflicts between newcomers and Chumash sometimes created serious problems. However, by working together, the Chumash leaders and the Franciscans managed to keep things going. The Chumash did not find heaven on earth, but they did believe that they would have a future in Spanish California.

A Turning Point

By 1810, the Franciscans ran the Chumash missions with the help of traditional leaders who had taken on the roles of mayor and city councilmen. Although they directed many of the Chumash's activities, the missionaries never imagined that they owned them, or anything else that was found in the settlements. To many of the Spanish, it now seemed that the neophytes had learned to live and think like Europeans. However, most of the Chumash did not forget who they were. They mastered the new ways but preserved many of their traditions, including their language and stories. Most of them adopted Christian beliefs but also maintained, with equal determination, their Chumash faith.

The Chumash of California

In 1822, the Chumash were shocked to receive word that Spain had abandoned its claim to California. Far to the south, in Mexico, rebels had won their war for independence from Spain in 1821. California, and the Chumash, were now part of the new nation of Mexico. Some Mexican political leaders promised them that they would soon be given complete control of their towns and other property. The Chumash believed that they were ready to govern themselves as equal citizens of the new nation.

This photo depicts Chumash survivors during the difficult period after the decline of the missions.

The promises of freedom and civil rights would not be fulfilled. Many of the soldiers and settlers living in the region were mad that the Native Americans had such beautiful homes, magnificent buildings, and other possessions. To many of the newcomers, the Chumash could never be anything other than lowly natives. After 1821, more and more settlers demanded that the Chumash work for little or no pay. The Franciscans were forced to give away to the army much of what the missions produced.

The Chumash could not understand why they were being treated this way. They went to the priests for help. In the past, the Franciscans had found ways to find some kind of justice that was acceptable to both the settlers and the Native Americans. The Mexican government put the army in charge of dealing with the Chumash. They had no interest in listening to the Chumash or the priests.

In 1824, the northern Chumash missions exploded in violence. Chumash leaders called the people to come to Mission La Purísima and defend the settlement against the Mexican troops that were being sent from Monterey and Santa Barbara. If they could hold out long enough, they intended to demand their rights as citizens and as free people. Most of the Chumash did not follow the call. Some decided that it was better to stay on good terms with the Mexican settlers. Other Chumash, who believed that the rebels were justified but felt that they could not win, ran away to the Central Valley. In a bloody afternoon, the troops from Monterey captured the mission fortress and smashed the rebellion.

Even the Christian Indians who had revolted did not want to hurt their Franciscan priests or give up their Catholic religion. Between 1824 and 1833, the missions partially recovered. However, the hearts of the Indians and the Franciscans were never the same. The population dwindled as Mexican officials moved to eliminate the missions. When the end finally came, the government was supposed to give the Chumash leaders complete control of their lands and other property. Instead, the Mexican settlers took almost everything that the Indians possessed.

The Chumash After the Mission Experience

After 1833, the Chumash became foreigners in the land of their birth. Some worked as cowboys and servants. Others were captured and forced to live as slaves. Many of them escaped to the East. Here they joined with other Native American peoples and organized raiding parties that captured thousands of heads of cattle and horses from the Mexican ranches. By 1845, it looked as if the Native Americans might drive the newcomers out of California.

Everything changed in 1846. The Mexican-American War ended in a treaty that forced Mexico to give up its claim to the region, and California and the Chumash were now a part of the United States. The Chumash soon learned that the new government was no friendlier to their cause than the previous one had been. However, unlike

Spain and Mexico, the United States had large numbers of troops and many more weapons. They believed that all Native American people should be eliminated or sent away. The California gold rush of 1849 attracted people from all over the world. Within a few years, tens of thousands of newcomers arrived to get rich quick. There was no gold to be found in the Chumash country, but the emigrants invaded the Santa Barbara Channel area in search of other resources. Most of all, they wanted the land that had once belonged to Native Americans.

There were never any wars fought between the Chumash and the United States. By 1846, most of the remaining Chumash population was already a part of the Mexican community. Although they had not been treated fairly under Mexican rule, they

The Treaty of Guadalupe Hidalgo brought an end to the Mexican-American War and put California under American control.

had been citizens with the same basic civil rights as everyone else. But the United States denied nearly all Indian people, including the Chumash, all basic human rights. In 1850, the governor of the new state of California ordered a war of extermination against the Native Americans. Laws were passed that allowed the government to imprison poor people and make them work without pay. The only groups that were regularly arrested under this law

were Native Americans. Wealthy people were allowed to rent Native Americans as workers from the police. Sometimes the Native American prisoners would be auctioned off in public, just as the slaves were during the days before the Civil War in the Southern United States.

In 1855, the United States government set aside a tiny piece of land for the Santa Ynés Chumash Reservation.

Although they could never go back in time, elders such as Fernando Kitsepawit knew that knowledge of the Chumash traditions would be useful to their children, and to everyone. To many Chumash and non–Native Americans, these people were great heroes. If they had not saved this information, it would have been lost for all time, to all peoples.

Only 99 acres (40 ha) of land belonged to this last remaining community of Chumash, which was considered an independent nation. The people who lived there were encouraged, and sometimes compelled by force, to adopt American culture.

By 1875, most of the Chumash realized that as long as they said they were Native Americans, they would be stripped of nearly all of their rights. Most of the survivors outside of Santa Ynés told the Americans that they were Mexicans. Although the Latinos were not treated fairly, they were not treated as badly as were Native Americans. The Chumash were accepted by many poor people who were Mexicans, because some of them also had Native American ancestors.

During these dark days, a few Chumash, including Juan de Jesus Justo, Fernando Kitsepawit, and Luisa Ygnacio, tried to preserve what they could of the old ways. Fernando Kitsepawit was typical of these people. He visited the few places on the ranches and in the towns where Chumash traditions had not died. He learned all that he could. When he grew old, Fernando shared much of what he had learned with anthropologists, so that the traditions could be written down for future generations.

Five
The Chumash Today

The few remaining Chumash struggled to survive into the twentieth century. During the last 100 years, they have fought hard to protect their civil rights. Along with many other Native American people, they refused to give up their dignity, or to allow others to define who they were. The people at Santa Ynés refused to allow the federal government to eliminate their reservation. Attitudes about Native Americans changed very slowly. By 1900, many non-Native Americans realized how badly the Chumash had been treated. Native Americans and newcomers worked together to improve the lives of the Chumash. Gradually some of the Chumash families began to speak openly about their roots. In 1924, all Native Americans were finally granted citizenship.

Despite all that has happened, many of the Chumash preserved their identity as Native Americans. Today Chumash culture continues to grow and change. Some experts believe that about 1,500 people who have Chumash blood live in the Santa Barbara Channel area. The only reservation for Chumash is found at Santa Ynés. It is the smallest one in the state of California. In 2000, there were 350 residents.

These Chumash girls are wearing modern ceremonial clothing that reflects many Native American styles and traditions from the United States.

The Chumash of California

The early Chumash left many landmarks. Native American words echo in modern place names, such as Malibu and Pismo Beach. Chumash art is admired and sought by people from all over the world. Museums located throughout the region proudly display Chumash objects. The missions that the Native American people built are reminders of the failed promises of the outside world. Despite their incredible suffering, the Chumash endured.

Today their descendants continue the struggle for justice. Some want to be recognized by the state and federal governments as Native Americans. Others want the return of at least some of their lands. Nearly all Chumash want to protect their sacred places from development. They also want the return of the bones of their ancestors that are in museums and universities. Some Chumash also want the return of all of their artifacts. Perhaps most of all, they want to be treated with the same respect and dignity as other groups of Americans. The Chumash are a living heritage with a cultural legacy that all Americans should value and acknowledge.

Grandfather Semu Huate, a Chumash medicine man, in Ojai, California.

Timeline

13,000– 40,000 years ago	The ancestors of the Chumash arrive in North America from Asia.
8,000 years ago	By this time, people move into the coastal area of what will one day be the Santa Barbara Channel area.
1000	Many of the particular patterns of life that are associated with the Chumash at the time of European contact begin to emerge.
1542	Juan Rodriguez Cabrillo reaches the Chumash area and claims it for Spain.
1769	The first Spanish colonists invade California.
1773	The first mission for the Chumash is established at San Luis Obispo.
1782	The military settlement of Santa Barbara is founded in the middle of the Chumash country.

1804	The last mission for the Chumash is established at Santa Ynés.
1821	Mexico becomes independent of Spain. The Chumash become citizens of the new nation.
1824	The Chumash uprising fails.
1833–1835	The missions are eliminated by order of the Mexican government.
1846	The United States conquers California. Native Americans lose their status as citizens.
1850–1900	Numerous laws are passed that deny Native Americans their basic human rights.
1924	All Native Americans are made United States citizens.
1960– present	Many Chumash become involved in the Native American civil rights movement.

Glossary and Pronunciation Guide

antap (ANN-tap)   The main advisory council of the *wot*.

anthropologist (an-thruh-PAH-luh-jihst)   Scholars who study cultural, social, and physical aspects of human life.

aqueduct (AK-wuh-dukt)   A man-made channel used to carry water.

bull-roarer (BUL-ror-er)   A kind of musical instrument that made a low sound, like a helicopter.

Canaliños (can-al-EEN-yos)   A term used by some early explorers for the people who lived in the Santa Barbara Channel area. This word is also used by some researchers for the group of Native Americans who lived in the region thousands of years ago and who were probably the ancestors of the Chumash.

chief, chieftain (CHEEF, CHEEF-tuhn)   A leader who receives special privileges and collects goods that he redistributes among his people.

clan (KLAN)   A group of families that claim to be related to the same animal ancestor.

clapper sticks (KLAP-per STIKS)   A kind of musical instrument that was used to beat out rhythm.

cosmology (koz-MAH-luh-jee)   A way of looking at the structure of the universe.

culture (KUHL-chur)   Shared, learned behavior.

Franciscan (fran-SIS-kin)   A member of a Catholic religious group started by Saint Francis of Assisi in 1209.

gentile (JEN-tyl)   A word used for non-Christian Native Americans under Spanish rule.

hearth (HARTH)   A pit used for fires.

hematite (HEH-muh-tyt)   A mineral that can be used to make red paint.

Hutash (HOO-tash)   A female Chumash God.

ksen (KIS-in)   Chumash messengers and spies.

manos (MAH-nohs)   A fist-sized piece of stone used to grind seeds on a *metate*.

metates (MEH-tot-ays)   A stone slab with a bowl-like depression used with a *mano*.

Michumash (MITCH-yoo-mahs)   A name originally applied to the people of Santa Cruz Island.

mission (MIH-shun)   In colonial California, a kind of Spanish settlement where Native Americans were to be transformed into Christian citizens.

mortars (MOR-turz)   Circular holes in rocks that were used to crack nuts and grind seeds into flour.

neophytes (NEE-oh-fyts)   A term used for mission Native Americans who were new followers of the Christian religion.

nunashish (NUN-ah-sheesh)   Dangerous beings from the Chumash underworld.

paha (PAW-haw)   The main assistant of the *wot*.

59

Glossary and Pronunciation Guide

paqwots (PACK-whats)   The leader of several villages.

pendants (PEN-duhnts)   A type of jewelry suspended on a cord worn around the neck.

pestles (PES-tuhls)   Cylindrical-shaped pieces of rocks used with mortars.

petroglyphs (PEH-truh-glihfs)   Rock art that is created by pecking the outer surface off of rocks.

pictographs (PIK-tuh-grafts)   Rock art that is created by painting images onto rock surfaces.

rock art (ROK ART)   An art tradition that involves painting and pecking decorations and symbols on the surface of rocks.

serpentine (SER-pen-teen)   A kind of stone similar to soapstone used to make jewelry and tools.

siliyik (SIH-lee-ek)   A Chumash sacred area found within a village.

sinew (SIN-yoo)   A kind of muscle that was used in making bows.

soapstone (SOAP-stohn)   A kind of soft stone used to making cooking utensils, beads, and other tools.

social structure (SOH-shul STRUHK-chur)   A way of dividing a community into different groups of people.

tomol (TOH-mul)   A kind of Chumash canoe made out of planks.

utopia (yoo-TOH-pee-ah)   An ideal community where everyone is happy and treated fairly.

wot (WHAT)   A Chumash village leader.

Resources

BOOKS

Blackburn, Thomas. *December's Child: A Book of Chumash Oral Narration.* Berkeley, CA: University of California Press, 1975.

Campbell, Paul. *Survival Skills of Native California.* Salt Lake City, UT: Gibbs Smith, 1999.

Malinowski, Sharon (editor). *Gale Encyclopedia of Native American Tribes.* Vol. 3. Detroit, MI: Gale Group, 1998.

MUSEUMS

La Purísima Mission State Historic Park

2295 Purísima Road

Lompoc, CA 93436

(805) 733-3713

Web site: http://www.lapurisimamission.org

This state park preserves the buildings of one of the most important and elaborate Chumash missions.

Santa Barbara Museum of Natural History

2559 Puesta del Sol Road

Santa Barbara, CA 93105

(805) 682-4711

Web site: http://www.sbnature.org

This museum has outstanding exhibits on Chumash history and culture, and its Web site includes a detailed description of daily life in a Chumash village: *http://www.sbnature.org/chumash/daily.htm.*

Ventura County Museum of History and Art

100 East Main Street

Ventura, CA 93001

(805) 653-0323

Web site: http://www.vcmha.org

This museum also has excellent exhibits on Chumash culture.

WEB SITES

Oakbrook Regional Park—Chumash Interpretive Center

http://www.designplace.com/chumash

Wishtoyo—Home of the Chumash

http://www.wishtoyo.org/main.htm

Index

Index